Wheel of Life

Wheel of Life

by

Rona Adshead

AVON BOOKS
1 DOVEDALE STUDIOS
465 BATTERSEA PARK ROAD
LONDON SW11 4LR

Printed and bound in the U.K.

Avon Books

London
First Published 1997
© Rona Adshead, 1997
ISBN 1 86033 471 7

To Marlene,
the first person to recognise and
encourage my potential as a poet

CONTENTS

Country Walk

Along the Shore

A Poet's Endeavour

ON WRITING A POEM

White hot
       thoughts sizzle from spirit to mind,
       a lightning fusion
       incandescent with inspiration.

Red hot
       molten mass, blending, coagulating,
       liquid lava flowing in obedience,
       channelled by an even swifter pen.

Cooling
       so large a sphere compressed -
       can created sun become marks on paper?
       I burn, shrivel at my audacity.

Stone cold
       I am left with heaps of ash
       sifted by dry thoughts and dryer pen,
       my sun reduced to lifelessness ...
               another time?

EXPECTATION

Envelopes released like homing pigeons
from their nesting box of
      typewriter ...
            word processor ...
                  computer ...
flight paths hopefully plotted
for fair weather, straight
to editorial desks.

Or will their fragile paper wings
founder in thunderstorms of rejection?
Or perish on their postal journey,
fate forever unknown?

THE ONE THAT GOT AWAY

My mind leans over the bridge
linking thought and spirit.
Lazily I contemplate deep
pools of subconsciousness.

Unexpected inspiration flashes,
breaks the surface. The big one!
Oh, I recognise it - sleek and plump.
A world best seller. Nothing less.

With breathless care I cast
the rod of my pen, dangling
wordplay's sure bait.
A nibble, a bite! This is it.

Deftly I reel in frantic scribble -
reverent concentration shatters
hearing the too-well-known cry,
"Is there ANYTHING to feed the cat?"

Alas, my champion prize unhooks;
in agony I try again an empty line,
then console myself that even a
world best seller would not feed the cat.

POET'S PROGRESS

WRITING APPRENTICE

I offer these vignettes
as bon-bons
kept for special times,
like small surprises
pulled from Christmas crackers.
Maybe so am I.

CRAFTSMANSHIP

Such simple tools,
just pen and paper -
nothing more -
yet, linked by
hand, eye and brain,
may produce perfection.

THE CABINET MAKER

Poems are memory boxes
for treasured words
jewel-crafted by dreams ...
experiences ... passing moments
securely locked within.
But quirky recall
holds the only key.

My Country

NEW ZEALAND

These islands -
my inheritance -
where space runs free,
kicks up its heels
to reach the sky,
stands on tiptoe
to measure itself
against mountains
frowning in mock parental
rebuke at such frolics.

These islands -
my inheritance -
make water pistols
out of geysers,
see-saw on earthquakes,
slide down glaciers.
Please don't grow up
to match the world
for you are already spoiling.
So are your people.

OTAGO LANDSCAPE

Your paddocks jostle in mutual jealousy
competing for the fierce courtship
        of the sun.
Yours is not the green grace
that, mist cloaked, veils
virgin forest in modesty.
You have laughed with your
        lover sun;
shaken down your tussock hair,
brazenly blonde and bleached,
upon your breasted hills,
abetted by the wind's fine combing.
Then lay, compliant and unheeding
that drought will exact
        pitiless price.

CENTRAL OTAGO AUTUMN

I am far from home where
bush-cool bird song
still crescendos, filtered through
beech and punga, dappled
with sun or frosted with
coronet of raindrops.

Here heat wraps a blanket,
smothering harsh landscape -
poplars' burning spears
thrust savagely into sky
already scorched by
sun's lustful tongue.

Blood-beads of rowan berries
cannot placate by sacrifice
this ruthless ravishing;
nor dancing heat haze divert
by desperate performance
malicious nor-wester's intent
which joins in torment as it
blows still hotter,
mocks with choking laughter.

FROM EAST TO WEST

O brave the mountain passes
from Christchurch to the Coast,
let not the blandness
of Canterbury plains
diminish beckoning allure,
nor let the ordered web of roads
snare timid feet from adventure.

Steady on the slopes,
braking round the bends,
Tranz-Alpine train trundles on
where, cocooned in pea-pod carriages,
passengers are nodding to the rhythm.

Houses huddle close, chimney pencils
smoke shivering as they sign protest
about the cramping cold.
Skyline swings abruptly open,
silhouetted with autumn trees
throwing down gold leaf coins
in their hopeless gamble
against winter's coming blast.

Mountain tops, now bridal white,
seductively taunt a sullen sky
brooding in withered jealousy
over all this kindred beauty
which it cannot possess.

TAI POUTINI (SPIRIT OF THE COAST)

Westland's little streams
are amber brown and homely,
distilled cups of tea steaming
with mountain mist
risen from first sun
and redolent forest fern
to entice a drowsy tramper
out of sleeping-bag cocoon.

FRANZ JOSEF GLACIER

Capricious maiden of the Southern Alps,
moving eternally in nature's path,
yet, in contrariness,
abruptly changing at your whim
just to assert femininity,
we salute you with karakia,
finding foothold with respect
as we approach your flowing robe.

But, why, Nga Roimata o Hinehukatere,
does your resonant title mean
"Tears of the Avalanche"?
Is it because our pakeha tongue
was too impatient to learn
unfamiliar pronunciation?
Is it because homage to an emperor
was more casually bestowed?
He who was half the world away
and many worlds from your creation.

Nga Roimata o Hinehukatere,
humbly we restore your dignity,
requesting that you forgive
our pakeha obtuseness.

My Town

EQUINOX

Half gale northerly,
portending yet another downpour,
swaggers into town.

Wild West Coast sky soon
drowns in its own monotony.
Streetlights blink bravely
dodging torrential rain's
accurate javelin thrusts,
hurled in spite to slither
footpaths into treachery.
Sodden trees push petulantly
against the weight of water.
Depression makes its home
inside umbrellas, parkas, gumboots ...

But, as it is laughingly said,
"You can always tell the Coasters -
they never wear their coats."

STREET SCENE

Our street cascades with childish laughter,
betrayal of careless sneaking out
for forbidden final games
with bat and ball and B.M.X.'s.

Towards the west an alien sky
withdraws in smouldering resentment
that companion day has fallen into ash.

Friendly moons of street lamps
are suddenly alight as we stroll
through deep velvet dusk pricked
with last birdsong and first starshine.

Confiding roses, their incense bowls
burnished by twilight, cup
lavishly outpoured benediction.

LIFE'S RECKONING

Violet bloom of an autumn evening,
more delicate than baby breath,
diffuses hints of mystery
as it veils a subdued day
now considering its solemn end.

Business bustle's feverish spirit
pants its lifestream into restless sleep,
spent at last, wantonly or otherwise.
No time left now to redeem -
nocturnal hours bring their reckoning.

CHATTER TOWN

Sleepy houses slowly push aside
their eiderdowns of fog,
shivering beneath reluctant sun
while talking to each other
with rooftop smoke signals,
where icicles, eavesdropping,
start to wink at each other
as they pick up the latest gossip.

Rambling Round My Garden

OUTDOOR CONCERT

Song thrush on the lawn -
stage-strutting
beyond verandah's dress circle -
your speckled breast
a music sheet
presented proudly,
yet meaningless
to our human audience.

Your probing beak,
conductor's baton -
tuned and timed
with faultless accuracy
as your searching body
detects insect vibration
beyond the range
of our restricted pitch.

But we can at least
applaud your performance,
rewarded for diligence
with a wriggling beakful.
      Encore ...
            encore!

GARDENER'S DELIGHT

HERALDS OF SPRING

> Daffodils bravely pierce
> earth's dark scowl
> with their swords
> guarding fragile flower buds
> until they break into
> a fanfare of trumpets.

NAUGHTY GAMES

> Sun and shadow
> play dominoes
> beneath watchful trees
> betting on the score
> as they throw down
> their leafy dice.

NATURE'S SWEETS

> Popcorn daisies,
> nature's confectionery
> with sunburst centres
> sedate in paper frills,
> scatter over the lawn
> in a lackadaisical way.

Doors and Windows Opened

TEENAGE SKY

There is a teenage sky this morning,
budding from a hesitant horizon
daubed with lipstick streaks of sunrise
and awkwardly draping nubile hills
with tangled scarves of mist.

Youthful day begins, unsure of its shape:
but confidence comes with stronger light.
The sky pulls on its sturdy denim blue,
causing an anorexic crescent moon
to waste away in unseen pallor.

Suddenly a defiant shower
trips over its own sulky pout,
then, just as quickly, the sun
begins to poke holes in the pockets
of still quietly weeping clouds.

Oh, teenage sky, made of mood and moment,
take this as the morning of your life,
which is a beginning - not finality:
strength of noon hour is yet to be,
when you will glow in your fulfilment.

SEASON OF LONG SHADOWS

Early winter sun,
summer's last frail child,
clutches at the remnants
of seared autumn leaves
for scanty covering
as it peeps and tiptoes
to dodge long shadows -
malevolent cold fingers,
aged and shrivelled
from wind's cutting meanness.

Summer's last frail child,
born out of season,
indifferently cast aside,
wanders homeless until it finds
other maternal shelter
where it is nourished
to pour out its precious gift,
honey pale, honey sweet warmth -
spirit and body rejuvenation,
ease for aching bones.

WINTER EVENING

Winter's steel-tipped engraving
tool crisply etches the landscape
below late sun-ripened sky,
now dying passively in
the embracing harshness
of frost's foreboding
that has already frozen
the evening star's fire
into diamond hard brilliance.

Within My Home

BONDING

Patience with a child
is learnt from the child
when tired eyelids droop
after ever-bubbling play
and mischief on the boil.

Every exasperation
at the end of frazzled day
smoothes into tender smile
when gazing upon
newly created innocence
so vulnerably restored.

For trustful sleep never stirs
with open chubby fist
offering unquestioned love
to what should be returned
       in like love.

TICK-TOCK

A clock's voice never varies
filtering sands of time -
infinity ensnared
as tiny sounds
scratching incessantly
to escape the bonds
harnessed from day and night
by human ingenuity -
a simple dial, yet equal
to the sun's complexity.

TOSS AND TURN

When I cannot sleep
thoughts stray like
restless sheep nibbling
at the scanty pasture
of bits and pieces
left over from
the daily round -
monotonous stones
ploughed up by a mind
vainly seeking fulfilment.

I hammer down fence posts -
disciplined hours that
drop dark and slow into
the thudding holes
of my exhausted brain,
with minutes in between
strung like wire strands,
to try to corral those sheep.
      As if I could.

BLESSED HERB

So I take you to my pillow,
a sprig, spiked and stiff -
sombre green, rigidly upright.
What is there to commend you
to casual passers-by?

Your modest virtues are revealed
by touch alone -
lightest brushing with fingertips
releases aromatic joy,
soothing balm for wakefulness.

Thus I lay you softly by me
for intermingling of our breath
induces sweetest sleep.
When I rise, refreshed, renewed,
I bless you, treasured rosemary.

Within Myself

SILENT PLEA

Lay your gentleness upon me,
as balm for constant fretfulness.
Let it trickle down all secret ways
and labyrinth of my devious nature,
melting barriers of stubbornness.

Let your gentleness be tongue soft,
murmured patiently against my wilful words
when my vulnerability suddenly attacks
because my confidence shatters once again.

Let your gentleness be cape-like spread
to enfold me when bitterly sore wounded,
that, thus hidden, I may find myself again.
Let your gentleness fill up the holes
eroded by my caustic rebelliousness.

Then shall the scarring pit marks heal
beneath your outreached tenderness
until, like homing bird, I turn
arrow straight to you, secure
in the gentleness you formed in me.

CAT PROWL

Pain is feline,
padding purposefully
around the periphery
of consciousness -
poised to pounce
when its presence
is partly forgotten.

Pain, catlike,
rules the household:
it comes and goes
at its own impulse.
Sometimes it departs,
but mostly it stays.

Pain stalks its prey
with instinct
inbred for centuries,
immutable jungle law.
It stares inscrutably,
springs with unleashed claws.

Pain is as temperamental
as a cat, though house trained.
It can be lulled by warmth
until muscles relax
and the body purrs
with exquisite relief.

JUST A CRUMB

Often hope, freshly risen from
fermented dreams, collapses in cold
exposure of merciless reality,
slowly disintegrates to mouldy crusts
that block muddled mazes of memory
as convoluted as meshes of the brain.

Though deep stored beyond all knowing,
they may still be nuzzled
by thoughts scurrying like mice
meagrely nibbling around the edges
until dryness yields a crumb, enough,
just enough, to stimulate the mind,
rebirthing spirit's nourishment.

COMMITMENT

Commitment
>
> may be a millstone
> weighing down an
> over-strict conscience
> until dulled emotions
> wear into passive acceptance.

Commitment
>
> may be a grindstone
> lacking moisture of variety
> until the cutting edge
> of character is abraded
> down to duty's dust.

Commitment
>
> may be a lodestone,
> magnet for like minds
> that circle harmoniously,
> orbits never touching,
> yet stimulus for each other.

Memories

DANCE OF THE MEMORIES

Swirling,
     whirling:
image memories, dancing on the eyelids,
imprisoned fast, yet willingly captive.
Fantasising,
     tantalising:
how they retreat to shadowy past,
then suddenly flash to centre stage.
Elusive,
     illusive:
for remembrance is a puckish ballerina
who can cast mirage upon the truth.
Fretful,
     regretful:
because movements of the dance
miss beats unable to be filled.
Haunting,
     taunting:
that vagrant time tiptoes by
without a trace of choreography.
Fluttering,
     cluttering:
like fragile tutus crowding close,
bewildering in their variety.

And yet,
     and yet ...
what would we be
     without a memory?

HONEYCOMBING

I have built a hive
       of memories
for my brain is queen bee
       to attract them.
They swarm, cluster-cling,
       revitalise.
Then fly, bee-wing straight,
       through life's maze,
pollen-loaded with hazy
       detail to be distilled
as honey sweetness
       dripping down the years.

Yet, final choice is mine -
       will I allow memory to poison
       with one fateful sting?

HOLIDAY REMEMBRANCE

Those summer days rolled by
like amber beads strung
on the necklace of time.

But binding thread wore thin
through many monotonous years,
though I knew it not as I told
the rosary of my remembrance,
until it slipped from my
careful fingers searching down
dim corridors of recall ...
My amber beads are jumbled now
and most of them are lost.

What does it matter?
Still I hold a handful,
their preciousness intact.

ENCHANTMENT

Enchantment may brush by
as fleeting as a shadow:
yet, within a blink of time,
unsought and unbidden,
bequeath rare cameos
framed and fixed by the retina,
engraved forever upon the mind.

Most cherished are these impressions,
because they never can return.

One of the Family

SKETCHES OF MY CAT

DOORSTOP

Home stands
solid and welcoming
where my grey cat
dozes on the porch,
a heap of shadow
in the sun.

POSTAL DELIVERY

She then folds herself
until neatly arranged,
licks the stamps
of her serrated paws -
a parcel ready
to be posted.

OPPORTUNIST

Streaking inside
an unexpectedly opened door,
cupboard love rubs around
the fridge,
confident that another door
will soon open.

And the Neighbour's Cat

SALUTE TO SUNRISE

Silhouetted in early morning frieze,
next door's ginger cat
stalks along their garage roof
                    where,
caught by sun's first brush-strokes,
he transforms into a river
of molten grace ritualising
an altar, gleaming bronze.

Egypt's sphinx descendant crouches
with beryl eyes light-slitted,
lifts proud head eastward,
immobilises in timeless worship.

                    As I do also ...
                    but what - or whom?

Neighbours

FROM THE BACKBLOCKS

Morag is a raw-boned
lump of a woman,
with a jaw jutting
like a draught horse,
Life saddled her -
with a harness that chafed
her spirit sorely.
She pulled in rebellion
until dumb defence
learned to plough
ruts of routine
without conscious thought.

Her mane of streaming
dun-coloured hair is
skewered into place without
benefit of mirror.
Her hands are hoofs
brutalised through constant
grubbing ... milking ...
clothes and dish washing.

Morag is her own monument,
face etched with lines
giving away her story.
Her clothes are drab and
anonymous as a grave.

But the few people who now
drift around her town circuit
never guess that she
mourns not for herself,
but for her lack of children.

THE RECLUSE

He apportions his day
into neat little parcels
of activity.

> Each hour is a string's length
> to firmly knot his efforts,
> finally cellotaping
> with precise minutes
> lest an occupation comes unstuck
> and overlaps the next one -
> which will never do.

Only his address is missing.
Should there be one
when everything is for himself?

STAY-AT-HOME

She lived her life
like a question mark,
drawing half circle
        around her perplexities
        with wavering hesitation -
        can I achieve?

Followed by abrupt
downward stroke of
confidence shattered
        into the dot
        that ends the situation
        without decision.

SCHOOL LEAVER

Malinka -
      with her gawky gropings
      after graciousness,
      all giggle and gossip
      and hipswaying movement
      as she rolled her eyes.

Malinka -
      face framed with smother
      of coal dark curls
      tossed flirtatiously
      above lipstick slash
      while she rolled her eyes.

Malinka -
      curled catlike,
      careless of shoe dangled
      from foot and leg thrust
      below thigh-riding skirt,
      did she need to roll her eyes?

PASSING PARADE

GENERATION GAP

Boys develop foot skills
skateboarding rapturously.
Older men, bald men,
walk past circumspectly
for they carry skateboards
on their heads.

KATY DID

Katy's views were strong -
Katy never went wrong.
Oh, she couldn't
and she wouldn't
and she shouldn't
BUT SHE DID!

THE THINKER

His eyelids are pods
where dreams germinate
until snapped open
in fullness of time,
revealing bright seed
potent with destiny.

People with Special Needs

LOST WITHIN

Her eyes are palest green,
opaque, dimmed with age,
slow moving pools
fringed by scanty reeds
of her lashes,
scarcely illuminating
her lifestream consciousness
where her thoughts, like fish,
surface now and then,
too sluggish to rise
and take conversation's bait.

INTERVIEW

He had not been employed
for so many months that
he was worn down with
constant tramping ...
        smooth politeness ...
               shutting doors ...
                     empty mailbox.

But, now, once more,
(Oh, how many times
had he said, or thought,
"Just once more, surely")
he was ensconced
with an interviewer
who was second in command.

It was a little puzzling
but dulled repetition
failed to warn him
that the senior who withdrew
to sit alone
was the one to watch.

Be wary of the spider
in unobtrusive corner,
the one who weaves
assessment's web,
decision made from observation.
Do not chatter to his deputy
lest a job prospect is lost.

68

THE ONLOOKER

While I waited at a bus-stop,
a passenger alighted ...
manoeuvring steep steps carefully.

A girl - I remember nothing else
except her crutches, one leg in plaster.
As I half ran to guard her,
instinct warned me to watch,
not herself, but her feet.

As she swung down confidently,
yet carefully, I looked up
and was rewarded by her thanks.

When the disabled manage as best
they can, or propel their wheelchairs
through jostling crowds,
may they realise they are watched
not because of disabilities,
but in admiration for their expertise.

HALFWAY HOUSE RESIDENT

I know nothing of you, or your background,
not even your name ... do labels matter?
I first saw you with your bicycle,
all manner of bells and flags attached,
proclaiming your possession.

I hesitated to approach until I caught
a scornful murmur from those who should
have known better. That goaded my response.
I stepped towards you and was humbled
by your outgoing smile. Could I forget it?

I have just met you again, this time
walking with proud twirl of triumph
in your newest acquisition - an umbrella.
Without inhibition you called across the street,
"Only $9.75. And it's a larger one."

Your smile transformed disfigurement,
welling from innocence of limpid eyes.
Gladly I give you homage for your smile.

Country Walk

MUSTERING SHEEP

A farmer, eyebrows woolly, face weathered,
from learning harsh nature's craft,
knits his spun yarn flock
along the row of bitumen,
purl and plain, purl and plain.

       Keen-eyed dogs watch for strays,
       dropped stitches that unravel
       the pattern, purl and plain.

Patiently the farmer whistles
his four-legged workers into line
to safety-pin his sheep
between the gateposts while he
counts them, purl and plain.

       As they push each other free,
       crooked designs are drawn
       like a child's artwork.

At last the peggy squares of
sun-warmed paddocks are filled,
borders hemmed by fence posts
firmly hammered in.
No more purl and plain.

MOUNTAIN TRAUMA

All winter long
they humped themselves
against frost crackle cold:
bruised blue, shivering
miserably in tatters
of cloud and mist.
Soon ...
        too soon ...
will searing summer heat
rake their ridges
with relentless fingers,
scouring snow down
to exposed ribs.

SPRINGTIME MISCHIEF

Spring cracks on the pace -
an exuberant wind
seizes bare branched poplars
as broomsticks
to polish up the sky,
swoops to buffet pale sunshine
still winter-convalescent,
shrunken from its chill.

Ferns become busy hairdressers,
unpinning and grooming
dark curls of new fronds
beside a stream almost
splitting its banks with laughter
as it is tickled
by overhanging willow.

VALLEY VISTA

CHANCE MEETING

Cattle, with curiosity,
belied by torpid stare,
knuckle upwards
on lumbering forequarters,
prod forward, inspect,
return to ruminating.

WILDERNESS TAPESTRY

Hillside rivulets
daintily hemstitch
velvet moss cushions,
threading opal drops
to bind the fabric
that softens brutal boulders.

EVENSONG

Buttressed cathedrals
Of ancient oaks, sturdy
with time-tested roots,
cloister birdsong choir
where leaf and sky
pattern stained glass windows.

Along the Shore

IN SEARCH OF PEACE

Shell lying solitary on sand,
gleaming wet, newly forlorn
after tide's tongue-licked caress,
dare I intrude on intimacy?
Yet, compelled by compassion,
I stoop to hold you tenderly.

     My ear fits into your curve -
     ocean murmur makes us one.

Blinded by flash of revelation
I stare into sea's eternity,
catching truth to anchor
my ceaseless search for meaning
as war's heaving tidal waste
engulfs unto destruction.

     But fragile shell, though cast adrift,
     still cups inheritance of peace.

SECOND THOUGHTS

Yet aimlessly I ramble on,
so soon forgetting,
indifferent to the day -
warmth of sunshine
warms not my heart
as beachcombing fingers
drop discarded shells.
I face the inland climb
grudging every gravelled step.

Suddenly I glimpse
unexpected treasure -
the shore's creamy throat
modestly attired
with lace ruffled surf
where snuggles the bay's
greenstone brooch,
neatly pinned between
filigree edged headlands.

Ashamed, I turn
to retrace my path,
but all my careful searching
does not retrieve
knowledge I had thrown away
in self pity.
Could someone rescue me?

CLIFFTOP RENDEZVOUS

Would you meet me there, my friend -
wind expertly teasing clothes and hair -
where breakers pound impotent fists
against their inscrutable parent cliffs
while humped rocks transform
into ephemeral white staircases,
newly created with each upward dashing wave.

Would you meet me there, my friend,
run past foam's fretwork and climb
to watch sequinned shoes of noontide
go dancing on the bay,
rimmed by far reef's spray haughtily
drawing aside its seaweed skirts.
                Would you meet me there?

CURTAILED PICNIC

SAFE ANCHORAGE

Fishing boats, rocking gently
at anchor,
scatter like confetti
upon the wedding dress
silken sheen of
sheltered harbour.

CRUISING THE THERMALS

Caught in sunlight,
seagulls' wings,
exhilarated with sky space,
turn to golden pins
catching up the drapery
of net fine clouds.

HURRY HOME!

Out upon the horizon,
gathering storm
builds its anvil
on island smithy
where thunder hammers down
its lightning nails.